LOUDER THAN THUNDER

A CONTEMPORARY BUSINESS PARABLE

To Katie —
From the Drowsy

Listen and observe and you
are sure to meet with happiness
and success. Carol Dunitz

Advance Praise for
Louder Than Thunder

Louder Than Thunder shatters the glass ceiling while dispelling gender myths that have plagued corporate America for generations. This book is a 'heads up' for every businessman, an inspiration for every businesswoman, and a thoughtful reminder about how we can all aspire to be better communicators.

The Honorable Dennis Archer
Chairman, Dickinson Wright PLLC
Former Mayor of Detroit

Simple, straightforward and effective. Carol Dunitz has captured the essence of the important dynamics of human interaction.

John Bava
Partner, New York office
Deloitte & Touche

Louder Than Thunder is a wonderful book. Carol Dunitz addresses one of the most important aspects of communication… LISTENING! This can only be accomplished through something that is difficult for many…resisting the temptation to talk so much! The parable drives home a point that is a good lesson for all!

David Brandon
CEO
Dominos Pizza

If you want to get some tips on communication you might have forgotten along the way, or never thought about at all, pick up *Louder than Thunder* and throw it in your briefcase on your next trip. It's an easy read in a simple fun style. There's a lot of meat that you might not find your first time through it, but it's there for the taking. Reading it will be time well spent.

Keith E. Crain
Chairman
Crain Communications Inc.

Carol Dunitz has crafted a fine, captivating story whose lessons extend beyond the world of business into every walk of life.

Davy Rothbart
Publisher
FOUND Magazine

Even in the midst of a very demanding workday, I found that once I started reading *Louder Than Thunder*, I couldn't stop. The style is provocative and the message is compelling.

Sheelagh Whittaker
Managing Director
Commercial Sector
EDS Ltd., England

Louder Than Thunder

A Contemporary Business Parable

Carol Dunitz, Ph.D.

Canterbury & Parkside
Ann Arbor, MI

$\mathcal{C}$*anterbury*
$\mathcal{B}$**P***arkside*

Illustrations by Helen Gotlib
Design by Stephen Gertz

Library of Congress Cataloging-in-Publication Data

Dunitz, Carol
  Louder than thunder : a contemporary business parable / Carol Dunitz.
  p. cm.
  ISBN 0-9748659-0-7
  1. Business communication. 2. Communication in management. 3.
    Interpersonal communication. I. Title.
  HF 5718
  650.13

First Edition
10 9 8 7 6 5 4 3 2 1

For More Information About
Louder Than Thunder
Books and Learning Materials
www.LouderThanThunder.com

Dedication

My mother, my Uncle Dick, and my maternal grandparents were masterful communicators. My father was an outstanding negotiator. From the time I was in diapers I was constantly observing them and that is how I came to develop the interpersonal skills I have today. My children, in turn, watched my mother and me from the time they were small and have learned what I came to know. Passing the wonder of communication from generation to generation is very special. The goal of *Louder Than Thunder* is to share some of those secrets with you.

This book is dedicated in memory of Joan Mitchell Dunitz, Daniel B. Dunitz, Richard D. Mitchell, and Helen and Samuel Mitchell.

"It is the disease of not listening, the malady of not marking, that I am troubled withal."

William Shakespeare, 1564-1616
King Henry IV, Part II, Act I, Scene II

Contents

Index of Illustrations

Preface

Don't laugh. It was just over a decade ago when I was going through a divorce that I made an hour appointment for the first and only time to meet with a fortune-teller. My children were all in elementary school and one of their friend's mothers told me and another woman we knew about a Cassandra who she consulted from time to time. She told us the psychic was always forthright and incredibly accurate. Subsequently, we made back-to-back appointments to meet with this woman and drove over an hour to her apartment for the sessions.

In retrospect, what I expected was to be amused— and I did need amusement at that trying point in my life to balance everything else that was going on. Among other things, the fortune-teller told me she saw I would write books. This seemed odd because I had always seen myself writing plays. I started writing music when I was nine years old. In graduate school I wrote a musical for which I received an award. If anything, I expected at some point in my career to write for the legitimate theatre. I argued with her to no avail for she was adamant about her vision. Finally, I acknowledged that the script for a musical was often referred to as a book and that was probably what she saw. She shrugged her shoulders and proceeded with the reading.

A couple of years later I started a boutique marketing company, which offered comprehensive communication services. One key element in getting this type of business going is networking. I attended many events and on numerous occasions people would comment on my networking skills. I remember one man telling me that whenever he went to an event at which I was in attendance, he liked to stand by the side of the room and watch me work the crowd. It was early in my career and I naively questioned whether what he was telling me was a compliment or a criticism.

Around the same time, I started to attend singles gatherings occasionally. A friend who was also single, always marveled at my interpersonal skills and encouraged me to write books and give seminars to teach others how to improve their ability to interact comfortably. I told her the same thing I told the fortune-teller—that I wasn't really interested in writing books. Over the years, we would see each other from time to time and she would repeatedly insist that it was my calling. I told her I didn't think I would write a book on communication but if I did I would thank her in the introduction for her encouragement. Well, I have surprised myself—but not Jill. Thank you Jill Shapiro.

Since that meeting with the fortune-teller, I have completed a romance novel, which I may decide to publish soon. I have two books being published this year, the one you are about to read, *Louder Than Thunder*, and *One Hungry Child*, a book which I have written for the Food Bank of Oakland County to raise money nationally to feed the hungry. I also am writing a series of three books on business communication, which I started several years ago for which I interviewed many top executives. It is scheduled to be completed early next year.

So don't laugh.

Acknowledgements

There are so many people I would like to thank for believing in me and in this project. My children, Helen, Dorothy, Risa and Jocelyn, early on recognized to their dismay that I was not going to go out and get a 'real job.' They have encouraged me to follow my dreams much as I have raised them to follow theirs. Thanks to my daughter, Helen Gotlib, for the amazing illustrations in this book, and to my daughter, Dorothy Gotlib, for the artistic portraits of Helen and me for the dust jacket. Thanks, too, to Stephen Gertz for the hours he spent perfecting the cover and book design as well as the *Louder Than Thunder* web site and other peripherals, and Jason Mironov for the creative Internet marketing campaign he developed and implemented for the book.

I would also like to express my appreciation to my friend, Alan Barr, an astute organizational development professional, who always offers helpful words of advice and provided direction for the *Louder Than Thunder* learning guide. Thanks to my friends, Rhonda Cohen, who listened to each part as it was completed and provided praise and encouragement as needed, and Dr. Steven Steiner who carefully proofread the text before the book went to press. Thanks also to Joseph McMillan, Gary Corbin and countless other friends and business associates who have been supportive of me and this undertaking.

I am also indebted to all the executives I interviewed for the three-book project I referenced above. The insights they shared with me were invaluable and have helped me focus on important issues, which are included in *Louder Than Thunder* and expanded upon in the *Louder Than Thunder* learning guide. Many thanks to Shahla Aly, Steve Ballmer, J.T. Battenberg, John Bava, Robert Beggan, Richard E. Blouse, Jr., Joseph Braker, David Brandon, John J. Brennan, William C. Brooks, Patricia Hill Burnett, Philip M. Condit, Robert Cooper, James E. Copeland Jr., Keith E. Crain, Peggy Daitch, Joseph C. Day, Tarik S. Daoud, Richard E. Dauch Sr., Joseph DeLuca, Richard M. DeVos, Jr., Anthony F. Earley, Jr., Sid Feltenstein, W. Frank Fountain, Yousif B. Ghafari, Daniel Gilbert, Roger Goddu, Jody Graham, William R. Halling, David Hermelin, Mark T. Hogan, Gordon V. R. Holness, Patricia Ireland, Eleanor Josaitis, Chuck Kadado, Ph.D., Cleve L. Killingsworth Jr., Mary Kramer, Paul McCracken, Ph.D., Terry Merritt, Eugene A. Miller, Anne Mulchay, Timothy L. Nasso, Albert T. Nelson, Jr., Robert A. Nero, Stephen R. Polk, Paul W. Potter, Arthur T. Porter, M.D., J.D. Power, Heinz C. Prechter, Lloyd Reuss, William C. Richardson, Raymond S. Ross, Ph.D., Michael C. Ruettgers, William L. Schrader, Stephan Sharf, I. William Sherr, Linda Solomon, Barbara Stanbridge, Frank D. Stella, Kathleen N. Straus, Joel Tauber, Robert Taubman, W. R. Timken Jr., Linda Watters, Hon. Joseph A. Wapner, Kenneth L. Way, Sheelagh Whittaker, Larry Yost and Dieter Zetsche.

PART I

The Awakening

Once upon a time there was a little girl who was very determined. From the time she was barely out of diapers she was always trying to accomplish some new feat. One day shortly after her second birthday she accompanied her mother to the grocery store. On the way home her mother pulled up to a stop sign and heard her daughter yell 'pots' from the back seat.

"What?" her mother queried.

"Pots," the little girl replied.

"What are you talking about, sweetheart?" her mother asked perplexed.

"Pots, pots, pots," she shouted gleefully. "Pots, pots, pots," she repeated as she struggled to jump out of her car seat. She pointed to the stop sign with a sense of newfound pride.

Once upon a time there
was a little girl who was
very determined...she
was always trying to
accomplish some
new feat.

Her mother looked at the sign and realized that her precocious daughter had reversed the letters for 'stop.' That was why she was shouting 'pots.' She was only two but she was starting to read.

Later that year the little girl went with her parents to a large toy store. Her parents expected her to ask for one of the special dolls she had seen on TV. But the little girl showed no interest. Instead she focused her attention on a bright and shiny, two wheel bicycle. That bicycle was red with white pinstripes. It had multi-colored streamers hanging from its handles that captured her fancy. Her parents paraded her up and down the aisles. They walked through the whole store but the bicycle was the only item the little girl was interested in.

"Sweetheart," her mother informed her, "that bike is too big for you."

"What about that pretty tricycle over there?" her father suggested, hoping to distract her.

"I don't want a tricycle," she insisted emphatically, resting her hands on her hips. "I want the pretty red bicycle."

Her parents looked back and forth at each other and then at their daughter.

"Well, at least it has training wheels," her mother sighed.

"I don't want the training wheels," the little girl insisted.

"If you want to have the bike, you have to have the training wheels," her father told her.

"We'll see," she mumbled under her breath.

They took the bright and shiny bicycle home to placate their daughter, assuming she couldn't possibly use it for at least a couple of years. But when they got home the little girl immediately asked her father to go out with her to the sidewalk in front of their house so she could start to learn to ride it. She took his hand and he followed her with the bicycle in tow.

A week passed by. The bike was no longer bright and shiny. It looked like it had been through a war—but the little girl now liked it even more than when she first set eyes on it. The dings and the dents seemed to match the bruises and scabs on her small body.

She repeatedly whizzed down the block and back on it. The training wheels were nowhere to be seen. They had been tossed in the trash several days earlier.

When she was seven years old, the little girl spent her first summer at sleepover camp. Her parents had wanted her to stay home and go to day camp. She, however, insisted that she be allowed to go away like some of the older children on the block.

That year she beat out all the girls in camp for the lead in the camp musical. This was a very exciting opportunity. The campers in the musical would not only perform for everyone at camp at the end of the summer, they would also appear on the air when the production was broadcast over a local TV station.

There was a strict production schedule for practice. Every day the children who were to perform in the musical attended rehearsals. The little girl had to attend all the rehearsals because her part was so large. It meant giving up time swimming at the beach. It also meant fewer tennis lessons — but she felt it was worth it.

All summer long the little girl battled intense homesickness. Two weeks before the end of camp she was no longer able to control it. She got so upset she had to leave camp and go home. Her understudy was, of course, delighted to step into the lead role.

The little girl learned that the show must go on — whether or not she was part of it. It didn't matter how many talents and abilities she had if she didn't have the maturity to direct them in a constructive way. This was a very important lesson.

At age 10 she announced to her parents that she had decided to become president when she grew up. They looked at each other, smiled, and assured her that she could be whatever she wanted to be. All she had to do was constructively channel her efforts to accomplish her goals.

"Do you have any specific suggestions on how to become president?" she asked them.

"Get a good education," her father replied. "Nobody can ever take that away from you. A good education will help provide the stepping stones you need for achievement."

"Listen and observe," her mother confided. "Listen and observe."

The little girl went to her room and thought about what her parents had told her. She had already planned to get a good education. That was a 'no brainer.' But the advice her mother gave her, "listen and observe," that seemed less concrete. She wondered what her mother had meant by it. How could listening and observing help her achieve her dreams?

That night she lay awake in bed thinking about the kinds of things she had observed during her first ten years of life. She was confused about what to focus on and fell asleep as all sorts of thoughts, ideas and recollections raced through her mind.

When she woke up the next morning, she decided to attempt to follow her mother's advice. What could she learn by listening and observing?

At breakfast, there was the same excitement as usual. Her little brother who was habitually late came downstairs just before it was time to leave for school.

"Sweetheart," her mother addressed him, "there's hardly time for you to eat. You need to try to get downstairs more quickly in the morning."

"He stayed up late playing video games," the little girl reported.

"Ein wort weniger," her mother reprimanded her. The little girl had heard this advice repeatedly, first from her grandmother and now from her mother. The phrase translated from German as "a word less." Its meaning changed in different situations. Sometimes it meant—"if you have nothing nice to say, don't say it." Other times it meant—"it's better to be thought a fool than open up your mouth and prove it." Still other times it meant—"think before you speak"—because you often wouldn't speak if you thought about how others would react to what you were going to say. Her mother had counseled her that it was always easier to undo silence than it was to undo words.

At school that morning, the little girl listened intently to her homeroom teacher, who also taught English and Math. She observed that the teacher moved quickly from one point to another. There was very little class participation. Even when the teacher asked for answers from the class, few people responded. The little girl assumed that no one really thought the teacher wanted them to respond because she did not wait long enough before beginning to speak again. She wondered what the significance of this observation could be.

In the afternoon, her class went to Science and History in another part of the building. This teacher spoke more slowly than the homeroom teacher, and often asked for class participation. He waited patiently until responses were forthcoming. Sometimes the little girl became impatient with his presentation style and how much time he took between ideas. Today, however, she was intent on observing and seeing what she might learn.

More classmates responded — and when they did, their comments were longer. Students seemed more comfortable. They didn't simply spew answers. They took time to think about what the teacher had said and what it could mean. They reacted to what he put forth. And they drew some of their own conclusions. She realized that slowing down actually seemed to increase the quality of classroom interaction.

The little girl did not watch much television. However, that night a politician who was running for president was giving an address, which was to be aired during prime time. Her parents invited her to join them, which made her feel very grown up. She didn't understand all the references he made, but she did observe that he paused often and for extended periods of time. She did not recall seeing anyone do this before — but she knew he was an important and well-respected man. She wondered what he was up to.

The little girl observed that the politician only took long pauses after offering significant arguments or ideas. It gave his listeners time to digest the points he had made. It also made him look like he was very knowledgeable and in control. His style seemed to impress his live audience. People often applauded during the pauses he took. "He is conveying a message through the words he speaks," she thought, "but he is also saying something important when he does not speak."

Later that week, the little girl had a reprieve from school. It was "Take Your Child to Work Day." Her mother, who was an attorney, had suggested she spend the day with her. Initially the prospect of spending the day with her mother had not sounded so interesting. She had gone with her on "Take Your Child to Work Day" the previous year and they had spent the whole day at her office. It had been rather dull and boring. But this year her mother was trying an important case and had invited her daughter to go to court with her. The little girl was very excited about going to court.

"You must sit quietly in the courtroom," her mother told her. "Be attentive to what is going on and you will learn something from this experience." The little girl knew that her mother was right and intended to act very grown up. She was thankful her mother had not said, "Children should be seen and not heard." She had heard other parents tell their children this and never liked it.

In court she watched her mother and the district attorney question different people who took the stand. Sometimes the person who was being interrogated answered quickly and directly. She found this kind of response very satisfying and believable. Sometimes the person who was being interrogated hesitated or

It sends up a red flag
for me when someone
speaks and responds
at a certain pace - and
then there is a
pronounced change for
no apparent reason.

paused before responding. When this happened the little girl wondered what the person was thinking and why it took them so long to answer. Each person who was questioned seemed to have a certain pace at which they answered. What really threw her was when that pace dramatically changed during the course of questioning. One man responded fairly quickly to all the questions except one — which took him a long time to answer. She wondered if he was telling the truth.

As they drove home at the end of the day, she and her mother discussed the trial. The little girl asked about the man who waited so long to respond to one of her mother's questions. "Was he just unsure of himself — or was he telling a lie?" she asked.

"It's impossible to know for sure," her mother responded, "but it sends up a red flag for me when someone speaks and responds at a certain pace — and then there is a pronounced change for no apparent reason."

The following Saturday the little girl went with her father to buy some paving tiles. Her parents were doing some landscaping in the backyard and needed the tiles for decorative purposes and to separate different areas of the yard from one another. They had done a lot of research and come to a decision on which tiles they liked best.

Several businesses in the area carried the tiles and her father wanted to see who would offer him the best deal. He had already visited two of the three establishments to see what price they would sell the tiles for.

"I need 1000 of those rose colored paving tiles," he told the salesman.

"They're $1.35 each," the salesman responded. "That's $1350.00. Then there's the $50 delivery charge. That comes to $1400.00 plus tax."

"That's too much," her father responded.

"I could give you 5% off since you're ordering a large quantity," he answered without thinking twice.

"Across town they offered me a 10% discount and said they'd throw in delivery," her father countered.

"Fine," came his quick retort. "I'll match their offer."

"I'd like you to beat their offer," her father

When there is a
prolonged pause
following an offer or
counteroffer, the person
who speaks first is
generally the one
who loses.

answered.

There was a long pause that seemed like an eternity to the little girl. Finally, the salesman spoke. "I can't go any lower without approval from the boss. I'll see what he's willing to do for you," he said, and turned to head for the office.

"Do you think he'll beat that other price?" the little girl asked her father.

"It's almost certain," her father told her. "When you're negotiating, people often don't respond to an offer right away. When there is a prolonged pause following an offer or counteroffer, the person who speaks first is generally the one who loses. That's not to say they'll be losing, sweetheart. They'll still be getting the business—they just won't be making quite as much as they hoped to."

"The boss says we'll pay the tax on the sale," the salesman told the little girl's father upon his return.

"That's great," her father said. The two men shook hands. The little girl followed them when they went into the office to formally consummate the sale.

On the way home in the car the little girl asked her father about the deal he had made. "How much did you save?" she queried.

"You're studying math in school," he told

her. "When he went back to the office the price he was matching was $1215.00. Sales tax in this state is 6%. So how much did we save by asking the salesman to drop his price a little more?" Her father handed her a pen and some paper from his pocket.

"Wow!" she chimed after doing the calculations. "$72.90." It was quiet for a moment as she digested everything she had observed. "But was it really a good deal?" she asked her father.

"It was a good deal," her father responded, "because everyone was happy—or perhaps I should say everyone was a little unhappy. I would have liked to save more and they would have preferred to make more—but we both had a deal we could live with. You never want to take the last crumb off the table."

The little girl's parents alternated nights reading to her and her brother. The little girl loved to be read to and always begged for more reading time. That night, the little girl's mother read her a story before bed. When she finished the chapter, she bent over, hugged her daughter and gave her a kiss. "I love you, honey."

"I love you, too, Mommy."

When the little girl's father came into the room, he smiled warmly. He came over to her bedside, bent over and gave her a big hug and kiss, too. They did not say they loved each other that evening but they didn't really need to. Sometimes saying nothing means as much or more than saying something.

PART II

The Riddle

Years passed and the little girl grew into a woman. She quickly ascended the corporate ladder when her childhood dream of becoming president had been transformed into heading up a major corporation.

She was a wise and forward-looking CEO and president who for many years provided guidance and direction that helped the business grow and prosper. She instituted policies and procedures that ensured smooth operations and facilitated excellent communication throughout the organization. Her employees admired and respected her.

She sat on a number of for profit and non-profit boards. The CEO not only supported many charities, she encouraged her employees to work for causes they believed in. She even gave them time off from corporate duties to pursue charitable activities. She felt that this helped build character as well as goodwill in the community. It is no wonder that she was looked up to in the community and recognized as a leader among leaders.

One day she called her three vice-presidents in for a meeting. "Gentlemen," she addressed them, "I have been at the helm for a long time. Shortly it will be time for me to retire and for one of you to take over."

The vice-president in charge of manufacturing beamed. "Surely you mean me," he insisted, "since I have seniority."

The vice-president in charge of sales quickly piped in, "But I am the one who introduced all the measures that have dramatically boosted our bottom line. It must be me you are referring to."

The CEO looked at the vice-president in charge of human resources. He was attentive but remained quiet. Perhaps he was simply thinking that actions speak louder than words. In any case, he said nothing.

"I have given this matter a lot of consideration," she continued. "I have a riddle I would like to share with you. Whoever comes back with the best answer will be the next CEO and president of this company.

"That's a strange way to decide who is to succeed you," the vice-president in charge of manufacturing remarked.

"This must be a joke," exclaimed the vice-president in charge of sales.

The expression on the CEO's face belied nothing. She looked at the vice-president in charge of human resources. He was attentive but remained quiet. Perhaps he was simply listening and observing. In any case, he said nothing.

The CEO decided it was time to share the riddle. "What is louder than thunder, as highly charged as lightning, and more powerful than the fierce North Wind?" she asked.

"You can't be serious," the vice-president in charge of manufacturing countered.

"I will bring the best answer back for you," bragged the vice-president in charge of sales.

The CEO looked at the vice-president in charge of human resources. He was attentive but remained quiet. She wondered what he was thinking.

"You will have a week to come up with your answer. We will meet again next Monday at the same time. In the interim I suggest you take counsel with those around you. Try visiting

What is louder than
thunder, as highly
charged as lightning,
and more powerful than
the fierce North Wind?

different divisions of the company that you are less familiar with. Closely listen and observe. This will ensure you return with a thoughtful answer that is on point."

No sooner had the door to the CEO's office closed behind them than the vice-president in charge of manufacturing and the vice-president in charge of sales started quarreling about which one of them would be chosen. "This is ridiculous," the vice-president in charge of manufacturing barked. "What does she think this is? A television game show?"

"We'll just have to play along," the vice-president in charge of sales conceded. "As long as she's top banana we have to play by her rules." He then turned to the vice-president in charge of human resources. "You're awfully quiet," he added. Then he paused. "I guess you realize that you were only included to make it look like there is a fair playing field," he remarked disdainfully.

During the next week the three vice-presidents made a point of following the CEO's advice. They arranged to visit different departments at headquarters as well as plants that were located nearby. Each one saw the same things. Each one observed something different.

On Tuesday the three vice-presidents arranged to visit a large plant about fifty miles from headquarters. They were greeted warmly by the plant manager who offered to show them around. The plant floor was alive with the sounds of manufacturing. Stamping machines of all shapes and sizes methodically produced part after part. Operators attended other machines that cut and sanded and accomplished a myriad of other tasks. The din was deafening.

When they left the plant floor, the vice-president in charge of manufacturing expressed his concern about the noise level. "Surely there is something that can be done about it," he commented.

"Yes, indeed," the plant manager smiled and replied. "All of the workers wear ear plugs to protect their hearing."

"Of course," the vice-president in charge of manufacturing replied. "I knew that." To himself he secretly thought that he had found the answer to the CEO's riddle. What is louder than thunder, as highly charged as lightning, and more powerful than the fierce North Wind? It most certainly had to be 'industrialization.'

On Wednesday, the three vice-presidents
sat in on a motivational seminar being given
by the sales department to get the sales force
excited about several new products. The
presenter was masterful at getting her audience
involved. She demonstrated the new features
and benefits of the company's latest offerings.

The buzz among the group intensified.
Salespeople asked lots of questions and
boisterously showed their appreciation. They
clapped their hands loudly and cheered in
recognition of the new products and the great
presentation that had just been made. The
new and improved products were clearly well
received by the sales force, which was now
prepared to transfer its enthusiasm to the
customer base.

After the meeting the vice-president
in charge of sales addressed the sales
manager. "Are you always able to create such
overwhelming response at your sales meetings?"

"Yes, indeed," the sales manager
smiled and replied. "We do more than have
motivational meetings here. We have pep rallies.
It helps energize everyone."

"Of course," the vice-president in charge
of sales replied. "I knew that." To himself he
secretly thought that he had found the answer to
the CEO's riddle. What is louder than thunder,

as highly charged as lightning, and more powerful than the fierce North Wind? It most certainly had to be 'passion.'

On Thursday, the three vice-presidents attended some mid-level negotiations between corporate buyers and people who supplied the company with a variety of industrial paints. The buyers felt that the supplier was asking too much money for what they were selling. They were not willing to pay the price the suppliers demanded. Negotiations appeared to be close to a standstill.

"If we pay you what you are asking, we won't have any margin for profit," the buyers declared.

"If we sell our paint for any less, we'll lose money," the supplier responded. "This re-negotiating every three months is killing us. How can we maintain a reasonable production schedule if we don't know whether we'll have your business over time?"

The three vice-presidents listened and observed. They had the impression that the negotiators had reached an impasse. Nothing happened. No one moved. No one spoke. It was so quiet you could hear everyone breathing. Then one of the buyers started to talk. "Are you saying that you could make the deal based on what we've offered if we sign a longer term contract?"

Again no one spoke. The head supplier leaned back in his chair contemplating a response to the question he had been asked. He sat up slowly. "If you sign a two year contract stipulating we will be your exclusive supplier for that period of time, I believe we can come down to the price you want."

Again it was quiet but the tension seemed to subside. "I think we can live with that," the buyer said. The buyer and supplier smiled and shook hands. "Fill out the paperwork," the buyer continued, "and I'll see that it gets processed."

After the meeting, the vice-president in charge of manufacturing and the vice-president in charge of sales addressed the head negotiator. "Do you always spend this much time sitting around the negotiation table saying and doing nothing?" they asked.

"Yes, indeed," the head negotiator smiled and replied. "Negotiators need time to think, plan, and improvise their strategy."

"Of course," the vice-president in charge of manufacturing and the vice-president in charge of sales replied. "We knew that." To themselves they gratefully thought how glad they were to have already discovered the answer to the CEO's riddle.

Negotiators need time
to think, plan,
and improvise
their strategy.

On Friday, the three vice-presidents sat around a large table in the employee cafeteria. Several corporate managers they knew came over to join them for what they hoped would be a relaxing lunch.

"You really should stop smoking," the vice-president in charge of manufacturing told one of the men seated at his table who lit up a cigarette at the end of the meal. The man glared back at him but did not answer.

"The CEO is thinking about stepping down," the vice-president in charge of sales volunteered. There was a pregnant pause.

"Who is going to be her successor?" one of the managers asked. The vice-president in charge of manufacturing and the vice-president in charge of sales glanced at one another and quickly looked away.

"She's been a great leader," the vice-president in charge of human resources said. "Whoever she chooses will have a tough time filling her shoes."

"I heard you just had a lateral move to a different department," the vice-president in charge of sales commented to another manager at the table.

The manager felt uncomfortable and did not reply immediately. When no one else said anything he felt compelled to fill the void. "I'm glad they didn't move me up again so quickly," he said to save face. "This will give me a chance to learn another end of the business."

"Great contract you pulled off the other day," the vice-president in charge of human resources remarked to the woman seated next to him." She smiled back.

"Well, I guess it's time to get back to work," the vice-president in charge of manufacturing said, rising from his seat. Two of the managers stood up to join him. They consolidated what was on their trays and followed him to the area where cafeteria trays were to be returned.

The vice-president in charge of sales rose to leave shortly and was followed by everyone else at the table except the vice-president in charge of human resources who remained seated, lost in thought. He was considering everything he had heard and observed over the week. What is louder than thunder, as highly charged as lightning, and more powerful than the fierce North Wind? He thought he just might have figured it out.

Over the weekend, the vice-president in charge of human resources carefully reviewed everything he had seen and heard over the course of the previous week. On Sunday night he decided it would be prudent to discuss it with his wife. "Sometimes two heads are better than one," he concluded and she might have some interesting insights.

"What is louder than thunder, as highly charged as lightning, and more powerful than the fierce North Wind?" he asked her after dinner as he helped dry the dishes she was washing.

"Why do you ask me that?" she queried.

"It is the riddle the CEO posed last week. Tomorrow is the day when we must give her our answers. The response she prefers will determine who is the next CEO and president of the company."

"Hmmm," his wife responded. "What do you think?"

"I know what I think," he said smiling. "I've had all week to ponder on it. I want to see if you have some thoughts that would be helpful."

"I think the CEO is a very wise woman," his wife continued. "So much is riding on the correct answer to this riddle. It must be something very important — something that is at the foundation of leading a happy and productive life."

"I had not thought of it in those terms," he replied, "but I believe you are right."

"There is nothing more important than communication," his wife declared. "The CEO is an excellent communicator. It must have something to do with that. What is louder than thunder, as highly charged as lightning, and more powerful than the fierce North Wind?" she repeated thoughtfully.

"That's it," he replied. "There is nothing more."

"What can be sweeter than sugar, more bitter than horseradish or sour like the juice of a lemon?" she asked with a twinkle in her eye.

"Why do women always seem to speak in riddles?" he asked playfully, setting down the last dried plate. They smiled warmly at one another and embraced. He knew he was not going to get a direct answer from his wife and thought about the implication of the riddle she had responded with.

What can be sweeter
than sugar, more bitter
than horseradish, or
sour like the juice
of a lemon?

It was Monday morning. The three vice-presidents filed into the CEO's office at the appointed hour.

"Please sit down," she said, gesturing to an area where four upholstered chairs were arranged around a coffee table. She sat down and they followed her lead. On the table in front of them was a coffee pot, a sugar bowl and creamer as well as four cups and saucers. She offered the three vice-presidents coffee, which she then poured and served. "It has been a week since we all met together," she commenced, turning to the subject of the riddle. I hope you have given serious consideration to my query and have come back with some thoughtful answers.

The vice-president in charge of manufacturing began to answer almost immediately. "It was on Tuesday when we went to visit one of the corporate plants that I knew I had landed on the answer," he replied. "The sound of the machines and equipment all in operation at the same time was deafening. What is louder than thunder, as highly charged as lightning, and more powerful than the fierce North Wind? It must be 'industrialization.'"

The CEO did not answer immediately but took time to consider his response. "That's a very good answer," she said. The vice-president in charge of manufacturing smiled widely, confident that he would be the next CEO and president.

The vice-president in charge of sales, not wanting his adversary to bask in glory too long, began to share his revelation. "It was on Wednesday when we observed the sales department conducting a motivational seminar that I knew I had landed on the answer," he replied. "All of the sales force became so lively and energetic. They cheered as though they had been at a ball game. What is louder than thunder, as highly charged as lightning, and more powerful than the fierce North Wind? It must be 'passion.'"

Again the CEO did not immediately answer but took time to consider his response. "That's a very good answer, too," she said. The vice-president in charge of sales smiled widely, confident that he would be the next CEO and president. When the vice-president in charge of manufacturing and the vice-president in charge of sales looked at one another, however, their smiles faded. The CEO had indicated they *both* had very good answers. Whom would she pick?

The vice-president in charge of human resources recognized that the CEO was now directing her attention toward him. "And what answer do you have for me?" she asked.

"I have given much thought and consideration to your riddle," he replied. "All week long I listened and observed trying to arrive at an answer special enough to address such an enigmatic question. With every visit we made, I came up with new ideas.

"Finally I broached the question to my wife to see if she had some additional insight. Like you, she offered up a riddle." All eyes were now focused on the vice-president in charge of human resources. Everyone was sitting on the edge of their seats anxious to hear what he had to share.

"She asked me, 'What can be sweeter than sugar, more bitter than horseradish or sour like the juice of a lemon?' I do not claim to have the wisdom to use it to its full advantage," he responded with modesty, "but I think the answer to both riddles is one and the same—and I believe I know what it is."

PART III

The Answer

*T*he auditorium was full to capacity. Corporate employees at headquarters had anxiously flocked in early, hoping to get good seats. The CEO had called a general meeting to which they were all invited. It had been rumored that she planned to step down and select one of the vice-presidents to succeed her. They wanted to be present for that historic moment. They were also curious about who the new corporate leader would be for it would most certainly impact on each one of them personally.

There was a steady hum of conversation, which quickly subsided as the CEO ascended the steps to the stage and headed to the podium. Once there, she put on her reading glasses and quickly glanced at her notes. The air was still.

Anticipation was high. And all eyes were fixed on the CEO.

"Good afternoon," she commenced her remarks. "I am delighted to have this time to spend together to explore what is important to us all—the continuing success of this company. Ladies and gentlemen, you are the continuing success of this company. Without you, we would not have had the good fortune of achieving our goals in the past. Without you, we would not be where we are today. Without you, we would not have such a positive outlook for the future.

"A company is only as good as the people it employs. During my tenure here as your CEO and president, I have done everything in my power to demonstrate that I care about you. I have worked to provide you with a nurturing environment where you could strive to attain not only corporate goals but personal goals. You have demonstrated to me, to our customers and to the investment community that a work environment like ours, which promotes open communication and caring, will outshine the competition time after time after time.

"So indulge me, please, while I share some of my thoughts and ideas about communication with you. In years to come, I hope you will remember me as someone who left a legacy

of effective communication—an environment
where everyone is encouraged to contribute,
participate, and share. If I have succeeded on
this front, I will have accomplished what I set
out to do. I will be content to pass the reins on
to others who can bring additional assets to this
organization.

"I remember when I was a little girl taking
piano lessons. My teacher was not content
to have students who could merely play the
piano. She wanted to make sure we all had
a strong knowledge of the theory. Why was
that? Because she knew that you have increased
understanding and appreciation when you not
only do something but understand why you are
doing it.

"I was always fascinated with the notes
and the rests. You see, in music you not only
have notes that tell you when and how long to
play, you also have rests—which are notations
that tell you when and how long to pause.
Musical instruments like people need time to
breathe—and each breath that is taken has
meaning.

"Years later when I took a composition
class, I wrote a simple melody with notes and
rests. I turned it in to my instructor and a few
days later had a meeting to discuss it with him.
I had placed rests at the beginning of some

I hope you will remember me
as someone who left a legacy
of effective communication
- an environment where
everyone is encouraged to
contribute, participate
and share.

musical phrases and his immediate
response was to question it."

"You don't need to pause at the beginning
of the phrase," he commented.

"Yes, I do," I replied firmly.

"But why?" he questioned, looking
perplexed.

"Because it adds emphasis to the musical
phrase." I showed him by tapping it out.

"Oh, I see," he smiled as someone does the
first time they understand something new. "I
never thought of that before."

"Besides notes and rests, there are many
other directions in music, which instruct the
performer on how to interpret the music. Often
there are tempo markings, which—quite simply,
tell how slow or fast to play the music. If the
word, Adagio, is printed above the music, the
musician knows he should play slowly. 'Adagio'
is Italian for 'slow.' If the word, Allegro, is
printed above the music, the musician knows
he should play fast. 'Allegro' is Italian for fast.
There are other tempo markings including those
which tell the musician to gradually play faster
or slower.

"Musical notation also has symbols like
the fermata that tells the musician to hold a note
longer than it would normally be held. There
is an accent mark, which means 'play the note a

little louder,' and a staccato mark, which means 'play the note a little shorter.' Composers want to give musicians all the direction they need so they can interpret the music properly. Music has meaning. Not following the directions the composer supplies muddies or even changes that meaning.

"Perhaps you are wondering why I am taking the time to talk about music today. It is with good reason. You see, speech is like music. There are words or sounds and there are pauses. Sometimes we speak faster," she said speeding up, "and sometimes we speak slower," she added deliberately slowing the pace of her speech. "Sometimes we speak louder," the CEO raised her voice so much that she surely could have been heard at the back of the auditorium without amplification, "and sometimes we speak softer," she added in what was almost a whisper. "Sometimes we don't speak at all."

She gazed around the room for what seemed like an insufferable time. She was intent on having her comments sink in. "Often what we don't say is as significant as what we do say. A long pause may convey significantly more than words.

"An interlude when nothing is spoken can evoke emotion, intrigue, and curiosity. It can underscore tension, embarrassment, fear and

Musical instruments,
like people, need time
to breathe - and each
breath that is taken
has meaning.

conflict. In context, it can be used to question, promise, threaten, and forbid. Sometimes the best way for us to deal with the unspeakable is quite simply not to speak.

"Suppose you have a close friend who is moving away. You don't know when you will see each other again. You might be teary-eyed. You might be sad. You might be thinking about what it will be like without your frequent get-togethers. Perhaps you hug in parting. Will you both be talking extensively about how you are feeling? Probably not. You will most likely let the lack of words speak — for what can you really say at a time like that?

"On the other hand, there are times when you don't speak because that is the expectation. Suppose a subordinate comes into your office to deliver some papers to you. You might thank him — or if you are busy with something, simply nod. He, in turn, might just nod back. Here the lack of words defines the relationship. A subordinate often shows respect by letting his boss speak first. Status has its privileges.

"Speaking of expectations...we all have them. However, it is important to remember that just because we expect others to behave in a way that mirrors how we would behave in a given situation does not mean they will. Expecting others to behave in a certain way and

being upset when they do not is a function of
that misguided expectation.

"I knew two women who were very close
friends. One slighted the other—most probably
without intending to—but the result was a
major row, which all but ended the friendship.
Others tried to intercede but mending fences
immediately following the emotional argument
was not possible.

"Months passed and ultimately they
reconciled their differences. How did this come
to pass? It was not because more angry words
were spoken about the subject. It was not
because more apologetic words were offered.
No more words on the subject were exchanged.
The woman who had hurt her friend's feelings
always smiled and tried to convey warmth and
concern when their paths crossed. The other
communicated a coldness that demonstrated
she wanted to wound her friend—perhaps in
retaliation—and maintain distance.

"These feelings did not have to be talked
about. They could be sensed. Ultimately the
warmth and good humor of the former melted
the icy façade of the latter. And so, in this
instance, a lack of verbal communication healed
a wound. There are other instances when failure
to speak can inflict or intensify a wound.

"There are also times when failure to

speak may result in the understanding that a judgment has been passed. How many women in the audience have gone out, bought a new outfit and later, all excited, put it on to show your husband or boyfriend? I see a lot of hands. In this situation, will your husband or boyfriend always tell you what they think?

"Some of you are laughing. I think that must mean they will not always be forthright. Sometimes it is better to say nothing—even if it is interpreted as negative—than say something that offends. It is easier to undo the harm than if it had been inflicted with words. At the same time, the lack of verbal responsiveness to the outfit can be interpreted as positive—especially if it is accompanied by a nod and a smile.

"Sometimes people won't for various reasons be inclined to let you know that they favor or disfavor something. They may smile or scowl or maintain a poker face—which leaves it up to you to figure out what is meant. It could mean assent or dissent, favor or disfavor, pleasure or displeasure. Usually, you can figure it out—unless someone wants to be purposely enigmatic.

"Sometimes you can mislead someone when you remain quiet and do not respond. Suppose your boss asks you to do something by a certain time. When you meet later, he says, 'I assume you took care of that,' pauses and then continues with what he has to say. Your lack of a verbal response is probably interpreted as an affirmative answer. If you did, indeed, do what was asked of you, his interpretation is correct. If, however, you put the assignment off and have not completed it—you have deluded him by not directly answering.

"Did you ever notice that women pause more than men do—or that people from some cultures pause more than people from others? Here is the United States we generally prefer a quicker style of speech with fewer pauses. Excessive pausing often negatively impacts on our perception of others.

"In some other cultures, on the other hand, speech is seen as an excuse to delay action. Here, if you make an offer during business negotiations, you expect an answer— almost immediately. In Japan, it is considered a sign of respect not to answer right away and demonstrates you are giving the offer careful consideration. To answer too quickly might offend. We must learn to treasure periods where no one speaks.

"Does an extended period of quiet when someone does not respond necessarily mean something? It often carries a great deal of meaning with it—but sometimes someone could

Sometimes people won't for various
reasons be inclined to let you know
that they favor or disfavor something.
They may smile or scowl or maintain a
poker face - which leaves it up to you
to figure out what is meant.

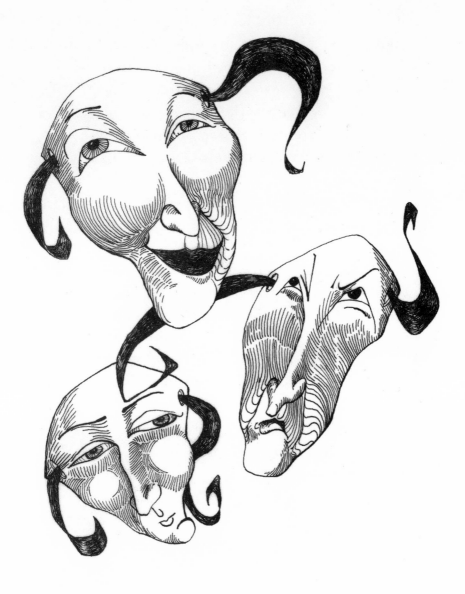

merely be lost in thought — or daydreaming."
The CEO smiled and let out an almost inaudible
laugh. "Well, I guess that means something, too.

"Several weeks ago, I posed a riddle to
your three vice-presidents and told them that
whoever came back with the best answer would
succeed me here when I step down shortly. I
know that such news travels fast along the
corporate grapevine — but for those of you who
may have missed it, the riddle is: What is louder
than thunder, as highly charged as lightning, and
more powerful than the fierce North Wind?

"Many of you have shared some thought-
provoking answers to the riddle with me.
Thank you for taking the time to participate
in the quest for something very special. The
three vice-presidents have also given me their
answers. It is now time for me to share them
with you.

"What is louder than thunder, as highly
charged as lightning, and more powerful than
the fierce North Wind? The vice-president in
charge of manufacturing, after visiting one of
our plants with the deafening sound of machines
and equipment all in operation at the same time,
told me the answer was 'industrialization.' This
is a very good answer."

The people in the audience listened
intently. They wanted to hear the answers

each of the vice-presidents gave and judge for
themselves which had provided the best answer.
But more than that, they wanted to know who
would be the new CEO.

Hoping to build anticipation, the CEO
repeated the riddle. "What is louder than
thunder, as highly charged as lightning, and
more powerful than the fierce North Wind? The
vice-president in charge of sales," she continued,
"after visiting an in-house motivational
seminar where the sales force became lively
and energetic, concluded that the answer was
'passion.' This, too, is a very good answer."

A handful of employees applauded,
demonstrating their approval of this answer.
Most people in the audience remained quiet,
however. The momentum was building and they
wanted to know who would be the new CEO.

"What is louder than thunder, as highly
charged as lightning, and more powerful than
the fierce North Wind?" The CEO paused. The
vice-president in charge of human resources
told me about all the people and things he had
observed during the week in which he was to
come up with the answer. He shared a riddle
that his wife gave him in response to mine.
'What can be sweeter than sugar, more bitter
than horseradish or sour like the juice of a
lemon?' And then he responded with humility,

'I do not claim to have the wisdom to use it to its full advantage but I believe I know what it is.' His answer was 'silence.'"

The audience was dumbstruck. No one responded. The CEO let her eyes cascade across the room. Before her she saw face after face devoid of expression. Everyone was universally fond of the vice-president in charge of human resources, but they were perplexed by his answer. How could silence be the answer to the riddle? How could he throw away his chance of heading up the company by telling the CEO that 'silence' was the answer?

As they sat quietly in their seats, people started thinking about everything they had just heard the CEO say. They thought about music—music they liked. Some thought about their favorite piece of classical music while others thought about rock or country or jazz. They realized that what the CEO had told them was right. Musicians did not play constantly. There were pauses when no sounds were emitted from their instruments. These pauses helped build emotion and develop meaning. They provided emphasis and created intrigue. "Could these pauses," they wondered, "relate to the answer the vice-president of human resources submitted in response to the riddle?"

The people started thinking about the

times they paused when they spoke to others. Sometimes it was to question something. Sometimes it was to demonstrate curiosity. Sometimes it was to threaten or forbid. "Could these pauses," they wondered, "relate to the answer the vice-president of human resources submitted in response to the riddle?"

They considered how their personal communication was punctuated with elongated pauses, which might heal or wound, express approval or disapproval, or speak when words could not convey all the feeling they had. Wasn't it amazing that saying nothing could have more meaning than rambling on? "Could these pauses," they wondered, "relate to the answer the vice-president of human resources submitted in response to the riddle?"

And then the buzz started. One by one people started turning to their neighbors. At first the sound of their voices was barely audible. Then the sound increased until there was a steady hum. The hum then escalated to a dramatically intense level. Soon the whole audience recognized the connection between 'silence' and the CEO's speech.

Several people rose to their feet and started to applaud. Others followed. Soon the whole audience was standing and exuberantly applauding.

The CEO raised her arms in the air and encouraged the people in the audience to take their seats. When everyone had quieted down, she finished her remarks, which at that point were all but perfunctory. Everyone understood the message of their CEO's speech. And they knew who was going to succeed her.

"Your next CEO is..." She paused and out of the corner of her eye could see the vice-president of manufacturing and the vice-president of sales glaring at the man who they had never even considered as their competition. "Your next CEO is the vice-president of human resources. He and he alone was not only able to observe others but also search inside himself to provide an answer to the riddle. His answer reveals a deep understanding of how we communicate with one another and how we might do it better.

"Speech is silver, but silence is golden."

About the Author

Dr. Carol Dunitz is a speaker, writer, producer and consultant. Her colorful presentations for which she dresses in costume include Schmooze or Lose, Leadership and Interpersonal Communication in the Workplace, Top Notch Customer Service, and Sure Fire Sales and Negotiating. She has written and produced numerous audio CDs to supplement her programs that teach audiences how to communicate more effectively.

Carol Dunitz is also a seasoned marketing professional who provides comprehensive communication services to business. She creates advertising campaigns that deliver formidable results by developing strategies and implementing them through high-powered writing and graphics. Among other things, Dunitz writes executive speeches, scripts, promotional literature, and web sites. She is noted for her ability to make anything interesting and easy-to-understand.

Dr. Dunitz has a B.A. in Theatre and English from the University of Michigan and a Ph.D. in Speech Communication and Theatre from Wayne State University.

About the Illustrator

Helen Gotlib is a prolific printmaker who works in lithography, intaglio and wood block mediums. Her printmaking and illustrations are highly imaginative and demonstrate a strong interest in exploring form and fantasy. She has traveled extensively in Japan, China and Israel. Her observations of people and customs across the globe have influenced her perception of the human body and how expressive it is.

Helen Gotlib received her B.F.A. from the University of Michigan School of Art and Design. She is the recipient of numerous art awards.

Louder Than Thunder
Books And Learning Materials

- Louder Than Thunder presentations and seminars

- Additional copies of the book, *Louder Than Thunder*, the easy-to-read book with a profound message for all ages. *Louder Than Thunder* demonstrates how learning to listen and observe ensures greater personal and professional success.

- *Louder Than Thunder* **(Book on CD),** read by the author.

- **The *Louder Than Thunder* Poster,** which features the *Louder Than Thunder* cover illustration by award-winning artist Helen Gotlib.

- **The *Louder Than Thunder* Learning Guide,** a study companion, which can be used individually or in classroom situations to focus on important ideas and concepts in *Louder Than Thunder*.

- **The *Louder Than Thunder* T-shirt**

For more information:
Visit **www.LouderThanThunder.com**

Notes